BATTLING BLAZES

Have You Got What It Takes to Be a Firefighter?

by Lisa Thompson

Compass Point Books ✦ Minneapolis, Minnesota

First American edition published in 2008 by
Compass Point Books
3109 West 50th Street, #115
Minneapolis, MN 55410

Editor: Mari Bolte
Designer: Bobbie Nuytten
Creative Director: Keith Griffin
Editorial Director: Nick Healy
Managing Editor: Catherine Neitge
Content Adviser: Randy Weingartz, Lieutenant,
        South Bend Township Fire Department, Minnesota

Editor's note: To best explain careers to readers, the author
has created composite characters based on extensive interviews.

This book was manufactured with paper containing
at least 10 percent post-consumer waste.
Printed in the United States of America

Library of Congress Cataloging-in-Publication Data
Thompson, Lisa, 1969–
  Battling blazes : have you got what it takes to be a firefighter? / by Lisa Thompson.
    p. cm. — (On the job)
  Includes index.
  ISBN 978-0-7565-3617-6 (library binding)
  1. Fire extinction—Vocational guidance—Juvenile literature. 2. Fire prevention—Juvenile literature.
3. Fire fighters—Juvenile literature. I. Title. II. Series.
  TH9119.T487 2008
  363.37023—dc22   2007032705

Visit Compass Point Books on the Internet at *www.compasspointbooks.com*
or e-mail your request to *custserv@compasspointbooks.com*

Table of Contents

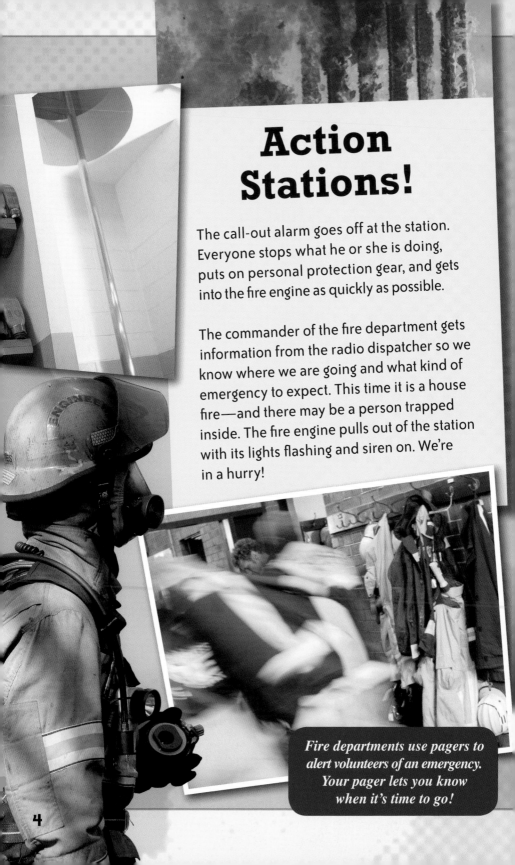

Action Stations!

The call-out alarm goes off at the station. Everyone stops what he or she is doing, puts on personal protection gear, and gets into the fire engine as quickly as possible.

The commander of the fire department gets information from the radio dispatcher so we know where we are going and what kind of emergency to expect. This time it is a house fire—and there may be a person trapped inside. The fire engine pulls out of the station with its lights flashing and siren on. We're in a hurry!

Fire departments use pagers to alert volunteers of an emergency. Your pager lets you know when it's time to go!

We drive to the fire quickly but safely. Emergency lights and sirens on the fire truck let people know we're coming, and to get out of the way!

We see smoke billowing out from a house when we enter the street. As soon as the fire engine pulls up, we jump out to make a quick assessment of the situation, while our driver gets the pumps started.

The commander calls the radio dispatcher to let him know we have arrived. The dispatcher confirms that a police car and ambulance are only minutes away. Together with another firefighter, I put on my oxygen mask, grab a hose line, which is a high-pressure hose connected to a water supply, and enter the house.

The house is black with smoke, so it's hard to see anything. Heat and fire are rising throughout the building. We have to move fast.

5

The Firefighter Buddy System

Firefighters always work in teams. The minimum team number is two. This buddy system helps the firefighters protect each other and ensures the safety of all team members.

My buddy and I search the house for the missing person. We find her near the back door. She is unconscious from the smoke. From her breathing, it looks as if she is suffering from smoke inhalation.

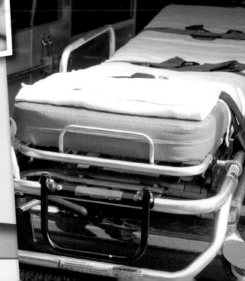

We carry her outside, away from the fire, and into the care of ambulance personnel who are now on the scene.

FIRE LINE DO NOT CROSS

The police have arrived and are blocking off the street as neighboring houses are evacuated.

My team drags the hoses around to the back of the house and starts to fight the fire from the outside. Water shoots into the house and onto the flames. Thick smoke is pouring out the windows as the fire grows. We will have to work fast to get the fire under control and stop it from spreading.

What being a firefighter is like

Being a firefighter is a combination of routine activities, intense training, and life-threatening situations—and those activities can switch instantly at the sound of an alarm.

7

How I Became a Firefighter

My dad was a volunteer firefighter, so I have been around fire crews and fire stations all my life. I grew up knowing the dangers of wildfires and the importance of fire safety from a young age.

Every spring, we would make our house as fireproof as possible. Doing things like clearing out gutters and removing flammable items (things that catch fire easily, like woodpiles, wooden garden furniture, and hanging baskets) from around the house was important.

PUN FUN Firefighters have to take the heat when something goes wrong.

One year, a huge fire raced through the area where we lived and destroyed houses on either side of us. It was very scary, but it made me see how important firefighters are, and the importance of educating others about fire prevention.

When I turned 16, I joined a community fire department as a junior volunteer. They let me become a full volunteer when I turned 18. The local station had great community spirit and there were always new firefighting procedures and equipment to learn. It was also a great way to keep fit, since we had training drills and organized lots of social activities.

Eventually I got a job with an industrial company and became its fire-safety officer. I took courses and received training in fire prevention and investigation. I also learned about working with hazardous materials.

There are lots of things to learn as a firefighter—and lots of things to teach! I guess that's why I enjoy my job so much. I really like being involved in fire education and teaching primary school students about the importance of fire safety.

The selection process to become a firefighter involves several stages. I had to take an entrance exam and participate in physical and medical assessments. There was also a round of interviews. Competition for places is so fierce it took me three attempts before I was selected—but it was well worth it!

I've been a career firefighter for four years. With more training, qualifications, and experience, I hope to become a station commander one day.

Firefighter training

Firefighters are constantly trained and tested in the use of fire equipment (extension ladders, breathing apparatus, pumps), handling hazardous materials, and fire science and behavior.

Qualities needed to be a good firefighter:

✓ mental alertness
✓ self-discipline
✓ courage
✓ endurance and physical strength
✓ mechanical aptitude
✓ ability to work on a team

✓ sense of public service
✓ ability to handle heights, stress, and confined spaces
✓ ability to assess risk quickly
✓ capability to handle trauma when working with accidents and emergencies

Firefighter Facts

• There are more than 1.1 million career and volunteer firefighters in the United States.

• Firefighters by age group:
  Ages 16-19: 3.6%
  Ages 20-29: 21.6%
  Ages 30-39: 29.1%
  Ages 40-49: 26.1
  Ages 50-59: 14.7%
  Ages 60 and over: 4.8%

• 13 percent of fire departments consist of all (or nearly all) career firefighters who protect 62 percent of the population

• 87 percent of fire departments consist of all (or nearly all) volunteer firefighters who protect 38 percent of the population

Life at an Urban Station

Firefighters work on a roster system. A shift could be 24 hours, with the next 48 hours off, or could consist of two 10- to 14-hour shifts with the next four days off.

Checking equipment is vital to ensure safety.

Daily shift timetable

8 A.M. Breakfast

9 A.M. Station duties—cleaning the station is an everyday job

10 A.M. Check equipment—truck, hoses, generators, pumps, breathing apparatus, air tanks, gas detection units, rescue equipment

11:30 A.M. Lunch

12:30 P.M. Inspect community properties for safety violations

1:30 P.M. Check uniforms—make sure clothes are clean and ready in case of an emergency

2 P.M. Drill—discuss gas detector and new procedures sent from dispatchers

PUN FUN The fire chief was always asked burning questions.

3 P.M. The alarm sounds—this time it's the real thing. We put on our personal protection equipment as quickly as we can and jump into the fire engine. The dispatcher gives us information like:

✓ the nearest cross street to the fire

✓ a map reference to get there

✓ type of fire, potential hazards, and any other important facts relating to the incident

3:10 P.M. Arrive at the scene—see there is no fire. The call was set off by a faulty fire alarm. While we are there, we assess the scene for fire safety.

4 P.M. Return to the station—recheck equipment and make sure everything is ready for the next call-out. The station officer writes an incident report.

6 P.M. Dinner

7 P.M. Station tour with local Boy Scout troop to teach them about fire safety.

8 P.M. Vehicle accident—check the scene for hazards and position the engine to protect everyone from traffic. We disconnect the battery cables to prevent fires and electrical accidents. Then we help the ambulance crew with the injured driver.

9 P.M. Return to station—recheck equipment and write reports

10 P.M. Time to rest ... until the next call.

Firefighter Gear

Advances in equipment and protective clothing allow modern firefighters to go farther into burning buildings. The equipment helps them stay in the buildings longer, putting out fires and rescuing people.

This gear helps us work among the flames:

- Helmet with visor and neck flap
- Flash hood
- Gloves
- Fire-resistant coat
- Fire-resistant pants
- High-pressure air packs
- Chemical- and fire-resistant boots

Who else is called to the scene?

Ambulance

Ambulance teams work closely with firefighters if there are people trapped or injured at the scene of an accident or fire. An ambulance team is made up of two paramedics. Paramedics are trained to treat patients involved in emergencies and accidents. They give medical care to patients at the scene and during the drive to the hospital.

Dusting for fingerprints

Police

If a fire may have been deliberately started or people have been killed or injured, the police are informed at the same time as the fire department. Police officers will put up barriers to keep people away from the scene, interview witnesses, and gather evidence.

Once the fire has been put out, the police arson squad will work with fire investigators to determine whether the fire was deliberate. If it was started on purpose, it is their job to find the person or people responsible.

Fire Facts You Need to Know

1 Fire is fast

In less than 30 seconds, a small flame can get completely out of control and become a major fire. It takes only minutes for thick, black smoke to fill a house. About 80 percent of all fire-related deaths happen in people's homes.

If you wake up to a fire, it won't be long before the whole house is engulfed in flames. You won't have time to grab valuables. A house fire doubles in size every 30 seconds. There is only time to escape. Just get down low and go, go, go!

9731-105 ST.

PUN FUN Some people find fire drills quite alarming.

2 Fire is hot

Heat is a bigger threat than flames. Just the heat of a fire can kill. Inhaling this hot air can scorch your lungs and melt your clothes to your skin. In five minutes, a room can become so hot that everything in it ignites at once. This is called a flashover.

Flashovers can cause temperatures to reach up to 2,012 degrees Fahrenheit.

Not just fires

Firefighters also go to the scene of road or rail accidents. They rescue victims or make the area safe after hazardous material spills or leaks from vehicles.

Cleaning up after a road accident with hazardous materials involved

17

3 Fire is dark

Fire quickly produces black smoke and complete darkness. If you wake up to a fire, you may be blinded, disoriented, and unable to find your way around your home.

Backdrafts

A backdraft is a roaring, explosive surge of fire that is produced when air is introduced to an oxygen-starved room—usually by opening a door or a window. The gases still in the room from a smoldering fire then explode. Firefighters must watch out for areas with few openings that have been burning for some time, because this could cause backdrafts.

Fire is trapped inside a room ...

... and then explodes when fed more oxygen.

Fire is deadly

4

Around 3,000 people a year lose their lives in residential fires in the U.S. The cause of death is usually from inhaling smoke or gas, not from burns.

Fire uses up the oxygen you need to breathe and produces smoke and poisonous gases. Breathing in even small amounts will make you drowsy, confused, and short of breath.

These invisible gases can lull you into a deep sleep before the flames reach your door. You may not wake up in time to escape. Most fire-related deaths and injuries occur when the victims are still asleep.

Back at the House Fire

Once the fire is out, we enter the house with a fire investigator to look for any possible causes of the fire. It looks as if this fire started in the clothes dryer. There is nothing suspicious, so the police no longer need to be involved.

After the fire investigator has finished gathering evidence for his report, we begin our cleanup. When we get back to the station, all the equipment we used will be cleaned (or replaced) and checked so the truck and the equipment are ready for the next call-out.

Where do fires start?

According to the U.S. Fire Administration's Statistical Report for 2006:

Residential fires are most often caused by:

cooking (26.4%)
heating (11.4%)
suspicious activity (5.7%)
open flame (5.4%)

Residential fires resulting in death are most often caused by:

suspicious activity (11.7%)
smoking (7.8%)
open flame (5.6%)
other heat source (5.1%)

No matter where you live, activities involving heat and open fire are dangerous!

In the United States, 1.6 million fires were reported in 2005. Between 1996 and 2005, an average of 3,932 Americans were killed and another 20,928 were injured as the result of fires each year.

PUN FUN A contest between two fire-fighters is called a "match."

Fire Specialists

Some firefighters train to become experts in special fields.

Fire investigators

Fire investigators work with the police arson squad. They collect evidence, interview witnesses, and prepare reports on fires in cases when the cause may be arson or criminal negligence.

A fire investigator carefully observes and interprets the smoke, heat, and fire effects to track down the place where the fire started. This is known as the area of origin.

Within the area of origin, investigators look for what may have started the fire, known as the ignition source. They identify all the potential ignition sources. Then, by analyzing test results, they rule out the sources one by one, until they find the fire's most probable source and cause.

Forensic fire specialists

A forensic fire specialist is someone who is trained in how fire works and behaves. Forensic fire specialists may work for the police arson squad or be employed by insurance companies, law firms, or businesses specializing in fire-related investigations.

For example, if it is assumed that a hair dryer is the ignition source, the forensic fire specialist must determine that the hair dryer really did cause the fire. He must also be able to explain how the hair dryer malfunctioned to cause the fire, and why.

Real crime scene investigators

Forensic relates to the application of scientific knowledge to legal problems. Forensic experts present evidence in court relating to their special field of study.

Some companies and industries have their own specialist firefighting teams. Most major airports have their own firefighting teams. They have particular expertise in battling fires involving highly flammable materials, such as kerosene-based jet fuel. They are trained to use equipment designed specifically for fighting aircraft fires and are also trained in aircraft-passenger rescue.

Fire-safety officers

Many companies train their employees to become fire-safety officers. As well as being trained in fire-safety procedures, these fire-safety officers undergo continual hazmat (hazardous material) training. Some take advanced training and become team captains to the regular officers.

Hazardous materials require particular handling and disposal procedures. This is because they can be highly toxic or flammable and may pose a threat to people and the environment.

Fire education
Part of our job is also to educate the public about fire safety and make sure people understand the work that we do.

Road safety
Firefighters witness the results of many road accidents, so they're in a good position to educate young drivers about road safety. They reinforce the real consequences of unsafe driving and encourage drivers to be more careful on the road to reduce the number of automobile accidents.

Playing with fire

Nearly 10 percent of all fires are believed to have been started by children. Therefore, it is very important for firefighters to teach parents and children about the real dangers of playing with fire. We promote sensible behavior around fire to reduce the terrible cost to people and property.

Famous Fires

Fires have always been a major hazard, causing great amounts of damage to cities and towns. Today they are still a huge threat to modern civilization.

Fire of London, September 2, 1666

The Fire of London started in a bakery and lasted for several days. It destroyed more than 13,000 buildings and caused nearly $2 billion in damage. Although buildings made with wood and thatch (roof coverings made of dried plants) were prohibited, people continued to use them because they were inexpensive. The drawback was that they were highly flammable.

The Great Chicago Fire, October 8, 1871

The summer of 1871 was unusually dry, and most buildings at that time were made of wood. Legend has it that a cow kicking over a burning lamp started the fire. It burned for 27 hours, destroying more than 17,000 structures and leaving 90,000 people homeless.

Triangle Shirtwaist Factory fire, March 25, 1911

This was the largest factory fire in the history of New York City. Hundreds of workers were trapped on the upper floors when elevators caught fire, the fire escape broke, and the doors to stairways were locked. In the 30 minutes it took for the fire to burn out, 146 workers perished.

The *Hindenburg*, May 6, 1937

The length of three football fields, the *Hindenburg* was the largest dirigible (rigid hydrogen-filled airship) ever built. It was designed to carry passengers over long distances. It mysteriously burst into flames 260 feet in the air. The crash over New Jersey took 34 seconds and killed 36 of the 97 passengers aboard.

World Trade Center, September 11, 2001

Nineteen terrorists hijacked four commercial airplanes and crashed two into the World Trade Center in New York City. The third plane crashed into the Pentagon, near Washington, D.C. The fourth was rerouted away from its intended target and instead crashed in a field in Pennsylvania.

The towers of the World Trade Center caught fire after the planes crashed, resulting in thousands of deaths. New York firefighters were overwhelmed and instead of fighting the fire, they concentrated on evacuating people from the buildings. More than 340 of these firefighters lost their lives when the towers collapsed. In total, there were nearly 3,000 deaths.

Even with a constant spray of water, the fires burning in the buildings' rubble took several weeks to put out. They continued to smolder for more than 100 days. It was the longest-lasting building fire in history.

The Tribute in Light marks the site of the World Trade Center every September 11.

Fighting Wildfires

While firefighters in city stations fight mostly residential and commercial fires, managing wildfires is a more community-based service. Rural fire departments are made up of volunteers who fight wildfires and structural fires, assist at crash scenes, and carry out search-and-rescue operations.

Dispatchers alert firefighters about emergencies.

Wildfire-safety measures include:

- Creating a wildfire-survival plan for your house and family
- Preparing water, hoses, and buckets to put out the fire
- Wearing protective clothes for fighting fire—long pants and long sleeves, sturdy boots, goggles, and gloves

FEMA Volunteers

The Federal Emergency Management Agency is a group of 2,600 full-time and 4,000 standby employees working across the country. They are in charge of assisting the public before, during, and after disasters such as floods, fires, tsunamis, severe storms, and hurricanes. FEMA also provides support to other agencies, like the American Red Cross and state-level emergency-management departments. In 2003, FEMA became part of the U.S. Department of Homeland Security.

FEMA's expertise is in returning affected communities to normal as quickly as possible. Much of its work involves securing damaged or dangerous property and providing access to property. In an attempt to standardize operations and communications between departments, all fire stations are now associated with FEMA.

PUN FUN

The firefighter who kept going back to college finally got third-degree burnout.

The Wildfire Danger Season

The times of greatest wildfire danger occur when there is a combination of extreme weather conditions (dry, hot, and windy weather) and a buildup over several years of dry twigs and leaves. Long droughts in forested areas dry out vegetation and suck up moisture in the soil and water reserves in dams, making the landscape fire-sensitive.

When the weather patterns bring strong, hot, dry winds and the temperature rises, the conditions are set for a dangerous wildfire season.

Ground fires burn slowly in logs and tree roots, usually long after the main fire has passed.

Surface fires are the most common type of wildfire, and involve the burning of grass, brush, and prairies.

Wildfire danger

All these factors contribute to wildfire danger:

✓ lack of rain
✓ low humidity
✓ dry vegetation
✓ wind
✓ high temperatures over long periods

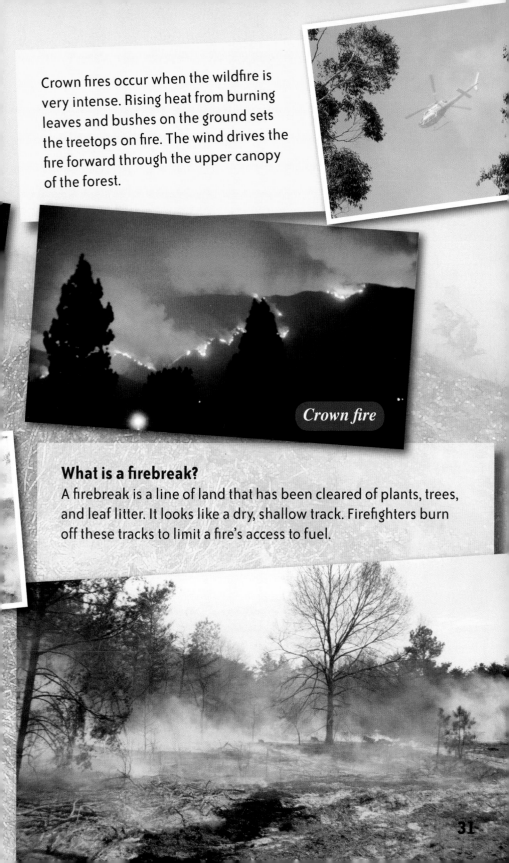

Crown fires occur when the wildfire is very intense. Rising heat from burning leaves and bushes on the ground sets the treetops on fire. The wind drives the fire forward through the upper canopy of the forest.

Crown fire

What is a firebreak?

A firebreak is a line of land that has been cleared of plants, trees, and leaf litter. It looks like a dry, shallow track. Firefighters burn off these tracks to limit a fire's access to fuel.

Danger Signs

During the wildfire season, fire officials calculate the maximum fire danger for each day. This helps fire authorities predict the probable behavior of a fire. The warnings refer to the chance of a fire's starting, how fast it will spread, and the projected difficulty of keeping it under control.

Wildfire danger levels		
Green		low
Light blue		moderate
Yellow		high
Orange		very high
Red		extreme

On days of high to extreme danger, fire authorities may declare a fire ban and put firefighters on standby in case of a fire outbreak. A "preparedness level" system might be used to track wildfire activity and resource use.

Preparedness levels	
Level 1:	No large fire activity, low to moderate fire danger
Level 2:	High fire danger in one geographic area; potential of becoming a large fire. Possibility of moving available resources to this area.
Level 3:	Two or more geographic areas experiencing significant fire activity. Major commitment of additional resources needed.
Level 4:	Two or more geographic areas experiencing fires. Requires highest level of command teams to area. Competition for resources among several geographic areas.
Level 5:	Several geographic areas experiencing major incidents. Potential to exhaust all available fire resources.

The Fire Triangle

Three elements are needed for a fire to start and spread:

Fuel (to feed the flames): anything that can burn—can be solid, liquid, or gas

Air (for it to breathe): fire needs oxygen, and wind provides this oxygen

Heat (for it to continue to burn): dries out the fuel until it is hot enough to burn

This is called the fire triangle. Remove one of the three elements and the fire will go out. Fire authorities use the fire triangle and information about the type of fire, the weather conditions, and the terrain where the fire is burning to formulate a firefighting plan.

- **Fuel**—removed by raking and back-burning
- **Air**—removed by smothering small wildfires with dirt or water-based spray or foam
- **Heat**—removed with water, making it harder for the fire to heat unburned fuel to its ignition temperature

Fire Speed

Grass fires can spread up to 20 miles an hour. There is more available fuel in a forest fire—these spread more slowly, at a rate of around 9 miles an hour. The more intense the fire, the greater the amount of hot air that is pushed ahead and the faster it spreads.

Fires tend to move two or three times faster when they are burning up steep, timbered slopes compared with flat ground. This is because the flames are closer to the ground as they travel up a slope.

Because hot air rises, smoke and gases rising from the fire quickly dry out these trees and make them ignition-ready. The air and wind can also carry sparks and embers up the slope and ignite spot fires.

Wind provides oxygen to the fire and tilts the flames toward new fuel. As the fire spreads, the flames usually form a thin oval-shaped wall. The highest flames are at the front, which is normally the most destructive part.

A change in wind direction can turn the long sides (flanks) of the fire into a wide fire front and dramatically increase the size of the fire. If the fire is large and the wind is strong, these conditions can create a fierce updraft of air called a convection column.

This column moves just ahead of the front of the fire and can fan flames to heights of up to 650 feet. Burning embers are sucked up by the convection column and are blown ahead by the wind.

These embers can start spot fires several miles ahead of the fire front. This is generally how a fire can cross a road or a river.

A massive convection column

Special Wildfire-Fighting Equipment

Tanker trucks

Rural fire departments use a range of specially made trucks designed for tough conditions, like the heat and smoke of fire and rough, rural terrain.

Tankers for wildfires and grass-fire fighting are four-wheel drive and have low centers of gravity so they can work off-road or on difficult trails.

Since wildfires are generally also a long way from water hydrants, dams, or rivers, these tankers are equipped with large water tanks. These tanks have pumps that can spray hundreds of gallons of water per minute. The average tanker can carry from 1,500 to 4,000 gallons of water at a time.

Fire tankers also carry thousands of dollars' worth of equipment, such as hoses, nozzles, chainsaws, drip torches, and breathing apparatus. Firefighters often need to take specialized courses in order to use the equipment.

Air tankers

Helicopters and fixed-wing aircraft are most often used for aerial firefighting. They are fitted with tanks or buckets for carrying water or fire retardant. In the United States, most firefighting aircraft are privately owned and are contracted out to government agencies. The National Guard and the U.S. Marines also have their own fleets of firefighting aircraft. Russia has the most efficient air tanker—the *Ilyushin-76 Waterbomber* can carry up to 11,000 gallons of liquid and can be filled and ready for takeoff in 15 minutes. It can soak an area as large as 12 football fields in 10 seconds.

A safer tanker

In 2002, five firefighters were killed when two air tankers crashed. The ex-military air tankers, which are used by the Forest Service and Bureau of Land Management, are not specifically designed for fighting wildfires. Some were built as far back as the 1940s. In 2004, all tankers were inspected and those not conforming to the standards were grounded. Other aircraft, like smaller tankers and large and small helicopters, replaced the tankers no longer in service.

Information from the Air

National Aeronautics and
Space Administration satellites
help scientists find the precise
location of wildfires in the
United States. This information
makes it easier to track the
movement of wildfires and to
predict locations of wildfires
in advance.

*A view from the air helps us
know where we're needed.*

NASA also developed the ER-2, an aircraft designed for data
collection. The ER-2 flies at an altitude of 60,000 feet and can
provide firefighters with color, infrared, and thermal images
of wildfire activity.

Radar

NASA's SeaWinds radar scatterometer is
capable of measuring wind velocity in any
weather condition. It supplies
accurate high-resolution images
of its findings at rapid speeds.
This information is used to
predict the weather around the
world, and is essential in storm
tracking and climate research.

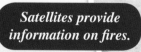

*Satellites provide
information on fires.*

When I was 19 and had been a volunteer firefighter for just over a year, I was put to the test when a wildfire started a few miles from our town. Here's what happened.

2 P.M. My pager goes off—I'm needed! I hurry to the fire station as the other volunteers arrive.

3 P.M. We're already in the thick of things fighting the flames; since the fire is so close to our town, we're working hard on property protection, standing between the fire and homes with tankers and hoses, putting out spot fires to save nearby houses.

5:30 P.M. Tackling the fire head-on, it's hard to breathe in the smoke so we're taking short shifts at the front. Other firefighters are making progress by creating firebreaks to back-burn later tonight to contain the fire.

10:30 P.M. Still at it. I feel as if this day has gone on forever. I'm tired and filthy but we can't stop now. Local people and volunteer groups are supporting us with food and water. Then fresh crews arrive, thank goodness!

MIDNIGHT It's 10 hours later and we're exhausted but happy. The danger has passed, but there's still a lot of work to do. Now we head home for a well-deserved shower and some sleep. Tomorrow we'll help mop up and make sure that the fire is really gone. Phew!

Become Your Home's Fire-Safety Officer

Fighting fire at home

There are various types of fire extinguishers. Be sure you know which types of extinguishers are designed for which fires. They are either marked with symbols and letters, or images showing the types of fires the extinguisher is approved for fighting. A red slash through any of the symbols tells you that the extinguisher cannot be used on that class of fire. A missing symbol tells you that the extinguisher has not been tested on that class of fire.

- **Class A: Combustibles**—for wood, paper, and cloth fires only.
- **Class B: Liquids**—for flammable liquid and gas fires (like gasoline or oil)
- **Class C: Electrical**—for fires involving live electrical equipment; these fires require nonconductive extinguishing agents
- **Class D: Combustible Metals**—for fires involving combustible metals like magnesium or sodium; these fires require an extinguishing agent that will not react with burning metal
- **Class K: Cooking**—for fires involving cooking oils, fats, and grease

There are also other powder and vaporizing-liquid extinguishers available for more specialized metal fires.

Know before you let go

Always check what extinguisher you have before using it. The wrong one could make the fire worse.

Top five tips for home fire safety

1. Install and maintain working smoke alarms.
2. Create and practice your home escape plan.
3. Ensure your home security lets you out quickly. Keep keys in deadlocks.
4. Be safe in the kitchen. Do not leave hot pans unattended and turn pot handles in.
5. Educate and supervise young children so they understand that fire is a tool, not a toy. Keep matches and lighters out of reach.

HOLY SMOKE!

A smoke alarm could save your life, giving you the valuable minutes you need to get out of the house. Follow these steps to have an effective smoke-alarm system in your house.

1) Test your alarm once a month.
2) Change the batteries once a year or when the low-battery signal beeps. A good reminder is to change the battery when you change your clocks for daylight saving time.
3) Replace smoke alarms every 10 years.
4) Install an alarm in each bedroom of the house.

Be Ready for an Emergency

In an emergency, such as a fire, follow these steps to call for help:
- Find a safe location to make your phone call. If a fire is near your house phone, don't use it!
- Dial 9-1-1. You will be automatically connected to the appropriate emergency dispatcher in your city or town.
- Stay calm, and tell the dispatcher exactly what the emergency is. She can't help if she can't understand what you're saying.
- State the nature of the emergency and the exact address where help is needed.
- Stay on the line in case the dispatcher has any questions. Don't hang up until she does.

If you wake in a house where there is a fire, and smoke is everywhere, the best thing to do is to get down low and get out fast. Wait in a safe place outside for the firefighters to arrive. Never go back inside a burning building.

STOP! DROP! and ROLL!

If your clothes catch on fire, don't try to run away. This will only make the fire burn hotter and faster. Instead:
STOP where you are.
DROP quickly to the ground and cover your face with your hands.
ROLL over and over to put out the flames.

Creating a Fire Escape Plan

1. Draw a diagram of your house. Figure out several routes for escaping a fire.

2. Plan at least two exits from each room in your house (usually a door and a window). Make special plans for babies, young children, and elderly people who may need help escaping.

3. Agree on a meeting place outside where everyone in the family will meet.

4. Practice this escape plan with your family at least twice a year.

Follow These Steps to Become a Firefighter

Step **1**

Finish your middle school and high school courses, getting the best grades possible in all your subjects. Most school subjects will help you as a firefighter—reading and writing, computer literacy and typing, and math skills are especially important. Other useful subjects are the sciences, technical courses like mechanics and carpentry, and depending on where you live, secondary languages like Hmong, Spanish, and American Sign Language.

Step **2**

Continue your studies at college. Many colleges offer degrees in fire safety, service, and administration. Most firefighters must continue these courses even after being hired. Look for courses in CPR or EMT training through the Red Cross or volunteer fire departments. Also, physical fitness is important, so concentrate on weightlifting and endurance training.

Step **3**

Testing is a big part of becoming a firefighter. There is a written test, a medical checkup, physical and psychological assessments, and an intense interview. So get ready to put yourself through the paces!

Additional tips to follow

When you do get a job, remember that being a firefighter involves shift work and having fixed vacations. It will be a lifetime of learning new skills and practicing old ones. It is also an incredibly rewarding job.

Licensed to drive

You must have a driver's license to become a firefighter—and a clean record is a big plus!

Make the time

Those who want to become volunteers must complete 70 hours of training, take training classes in biohazards and terrorism, and complete fire simulations.

Opportunities for firefighters

Firefighters can work in a variety of jobs:
- Seasonal firefighter—battling wild-fires, working on fuel-management crews, and maintaining general firefighting equipment
- Forestry aide—working with fire crews, fisheries, recreational trail programs, or habitat surveys
- Wilderness firefighter—battling fires in national parks and forests
- Firefighting specialist fields—fire investigation, airborne fire-fighting, or teaching firefighting courses

Find Out More

In the Know

- In 2006, there were 1.6 million fires in the United States.
- Fire is the fifth-leading cause of accidental death in the United States.
- On average, U.S. fire departments respond to calls every 20 seconds.
- Firefighters are required to respond to all fire alarms. The average cost of responding to a false fire alarm is between $365 and $1,050, for a total cost of $800 million to $2.31 billion a year.
- The average pay of a firefighter is $20.37 an hour, or $42,370 a year. However, many volunteer firefighters are paid as little as $4 to $7 per call, regardless of how long the call takes. Some are paid nothing at all.

Further Reading

Ganci, Chris. *Chief: The Life of Peter J. Ganci, A New York City Firefighter*. New York: Orchard Books, 2003.

Kelley, Alison Turnbull. *First to Arrive: Firefighters at Ground Zero*. Philadelphia: Chelsea House, 2003.

Reeves, Diane Lindsey, and Nancy Heubeck. *Career Ideas for Kids Who Like Adventure*. New York: Facts On File, 2001.

Santangelo, Mike. *The Greatest Firefighter Stories Never Told*. Kansas City, Mo.: Andrews McMeel Pub., 2002.

On the Web

For more information on this topic, use FactHound.

1. Go to *www.facthound.com*
2. Type in this book ID: 0756536170
3. Click on the *Fetch It* button.

Glossary

arson—crime of deliberately starting a fire

back-burning—intentionally setting fire to trees or bushes to create a gap so a wildfire can be stopped

backdraft—surge of fire that is produced when air is introduced into an oxygen-starved room

biohazard—an organism or biological substance that may pose a threat to human health

criminal negligence—accidentally doing something that can cause harm

dispatcher—person who communicates with firefighters and police

drip torch—small torch used for back-burning

EMT—emergency medical technician

firebreak—area of land that has been cleared of plants, trees, and leaf litter

fire investigator—person who determines the origin and cause of fires and explosions

flash hood—soft cloth hood worn for protection of the neck and face

flashover—sudden spread of flame that can happen when an area becomes very hot

hazardous materials (hazmat)—dangerous materials, such as acid or chemicals, that must be handled with special equipment or clothing

ignition source—heat source capable of starting a fire

nonconductive—will not carry electricity

paramedic—person trained to give emergency first aid

terrorism—harmful acts against people, with the intent to create fear or terror

wildfire—uncontrolled fire, often occurring in rural areas

Index

Look for More Books in This Series: